This edition published by Parragon Books Ltd in 2015 and distributed by

Parragon Inc.
440 Park Avenue South, 13th Floor
New York, NY 10016
www.parragon.com

Copyright © Parragon Books Ltd 2012-2015

Written and retold by Claire Sipi, Anne Rooney, Ronne Randall, Anne Marie Ryan
Illustrated by Victoria Assanelli, Erica-Jane Waters, Dubravka Kolanovic, Gavin Scott,
Polona Lovsin, Gail Yerrill, Tamsin and Natalie Hinrichsen
Edited by Rebecca Wilson
Cover illustrated by Alessandra Psacharopulo

Every effort has been made to acknowledge the contributors to this book.
If we have made any errors, we will be pleased to rectify them in future editions.

ISBN 978-1-4723-5466-2

Printed in China

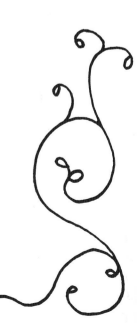

A Collection of
Stories for
4
Year Olds

PaRragon

Bath • New York • Cologne • Melbourne • Delhi
Hong Kong • Shenzhen • Singapore • Amsterdam

Contents

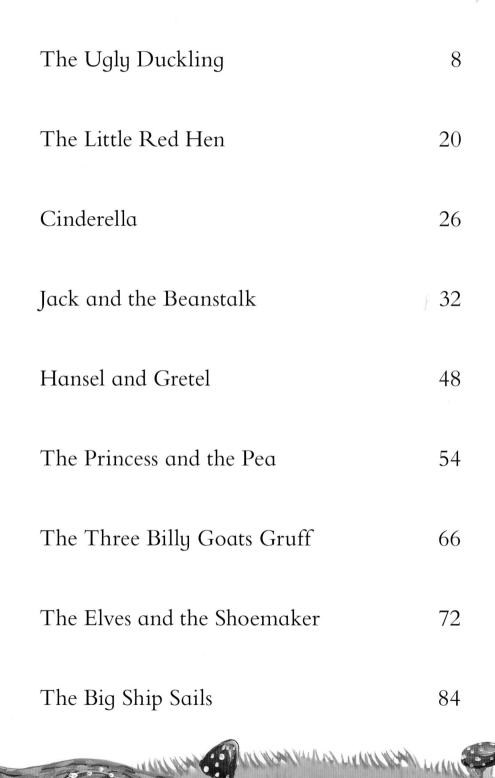

The Ugly Duckling

It was a warm summer's day and Mommy Duck wriggled excitedly on her nest. She could hear a tapping noise.

"Tap, tap, tap!"

"Quick! Quack! Quick!" Mommy Duck called to the other ducks. "My eggs are hatching. Come and see!"

One by one, the eggs hatched and out popped six chirpy
little ducklings.

"Ahhhh!" the other ducks sighed. "What sweet
little ducklings!"

Mommy Duck beamed with pride.

But the biggest egg of all still hadn't opened. And Mommy
Duck was sure she had only laid six eggs ...

Craaaaaaaaaaaack!

Just then, the final egg burst open.

"Oh!" gasped Mommy Duck.

The last duckling wasn't little, yellow, or cute. He was enormous, gray and well, ugly.

"What an ugly duckling!" quacked an old duck.

"He's not ugly!" said Mommy Duck protectively. "He's special."

The next day, Mommy Duck took all her little ducks to the farmyard, to meet the other animals. The six yellow ducklings proudly puffed out their pretty feathers.

"Ah," sighed the animals, "what lovely ducklings."

The ugly duckling waddled forward.

"Hello," he said quietly.

Everyone turned to stare at him.

"He's so GRAY!" neighed the horse.

"He's so CLUMSY!" mooed the cow.

"He's so BIG!" squawked the hen.

Large teardrops rolled down the ugly duckling's long, black beak. He felt all alone.

"Nobody wants me," he whispered. "I'd be better off swimming away."

The poor little duckling waddled sadly across the
meadow, leaving the farm and his family far behind him.

Soon the ugly duckling arrived at a river, where some geese were diving for food.

"Excuse me," the ugly duckling began bravely, "have you seen any ducklings like me?"

"No. You're the strangest-looking duckling we've ever seen," the geese honked.

So the ugly duckling waddled away. He was getting very tired.

As darkness fell, he crept inside an old barn, looking
for a place to rest.

"May I stay here?" he asked the animals
inside the barn.

"Can you lay eggs?"
clucked a hen.

"No," said the ugly
duckling sadly.

"Can you catch mice?"purred a cat.

"I don't think so," said the
ugly duckling.

"Then you're no use here!" the cat hissed.

The ugly duckling quickly waddled away until he came to a large lake.

"If nobody wants me, then I'll just hide here," he sniffed.

Fall came and the leaves turned gold. Then winter arrived, and still the ugly duckling hid in the reeds, too ashamed to show his face.

When spring came, a beautiful white swan paddled by the ugly duckling's hiding place. The ugly duckling backed away, afraid he would be teased.

But to the ugly duckling's surprise, the swan swam up to him.

"Why are you hiding?" asked the swan. "Come and join the rest of us."

The ugly duckling was shocked. Surely the swan must be talking to someone else.

But then he caught sight of his reflection in the lake.

He gasped in amazement. His gray feathers were now white!

"I'm a swan!" the ugly duckling cried happily.

Just then, a family of six young ducks waddled along the riverbank with their mother.

"Look at that beautiful swan!" they quacked.

Mommy Duck recognized her little ugly duckling at once. "I always knew he was special," she quacked.

The ugly duckling ruffled his beautiful white feathers, turned away, and proudly paddled after his new friend.

The Little Red Hen

There was once a little red hen who lived on a farm with a sleepy cat, a lazy pig, and a stuck-up duck.

One day, the little red hen found some grains of wheat.

"Who will help me to plant these grains of wheat?" she asked her friends.

"Not I," yawned the cat. "I'm too tired."

"Not I," snorted the pig. "It's too hot to work."

"Not I," quacked the duck and stood on one foot.

So the little red hen planted the grains of wheat herself.

All summer, the sun shone and the rain fell on the grains of wheat.

At last, the wheat was strong and tall with golden grains.

"This wheat is ready to harvest," the little red hen said to herself. "That will be a lot of work."

So the little red hen went to see her friends.

"I have worked all summer and the wheat is ready. Who will help me to harvest it?" she asked.

"Not I," meowed the cat. "It's time for my nap."

"Not I," snorted the pig. "I need to roll in the mud."

"Not I," quacked the duck, and she preened her feathers.

So the little red hen cut down the wheat stalks and piled them up neatly.

"Who will help me to make this wheat ready for the mill?" she asked her friends.

"Not I," meowed the cat. "I'm sleepy."

"Not I," snorted the pig. "I'm going to lie in the sun."

"Not I," quacked the duck, and she tucked her head under her wing.

So the little red hen beat the wheat to free the grains from the stalks and carried away the straw. Then she swept up the wheat and put it into a sack.

"Who will help me to carry this wheat to the mill?" she asked her friends.

"Not I," meowed the cat. "I need a rest."

"Not I," snorted the pig. "It looks far too heavy."

"Not I," quacked the duck, and she waddled away.

So the little red hen carried the heavy sack of wheat to the mill. The miller ground the wheat to flour and poured it back into the sack. Then the little red hen carried it home.

The little red hen was exhausted.

"The wheat has been ground to flour," she told her friends. "Who will help me to bake it into bread?"

"Not I," said the cat, ready to sleep.

"Not I," snorted the pig. "It's nearly time for my dinner."

"Not I," quacked the duck, and she sat on the ground.

So the little red hen made the flour into dough and put it in the oven to bake.

At last, the bread was baked. It smelled wonderful.

"Who will help me to eat this bread?" the little red hen asked quietly.

"I will!" said the sleepy cat, washing her paws clean.

"I will!" grunted the lazy pig, licking his lips.

"I will!" quacked the stuck-up duck, flapping her wings.

"No, you will not!" the little red hen said. "I planted the grains, harvested the wheat, ground the flour, and baked the bread. My chicks and I will eat the loaf!"

And they did!

Cinderella

Once upon a time, a young girl lived with her widowed father. He remarried, but his new wife was mean to the girl and so were her two daughters.

They made her do all the housework and sleep by the fireplace among the cinders and ashes. They called her "Cinderella."

One day, an invitation arrived. It was to the palace ball—where the prince would choose a bride!

Cinderella's stepmother was sure one of her daughters would marry the prince. So she made Cinderella work night and day to stitch their ballgowns, polish their shoes, and curl their hair.

But Cinderella longed to go to the ball herself.

Her stepsisters just laughed.

"You don't have a pretty dress, and you are always covered in soot and cinders!" they said.

Tears ran down Cinderella's face as she helped her stepsisters into their dresses and jewels. At last, they left for the palace.

"If only I could go, too," Cinderella sobbed.

Suddenly, there was a sparkle of light in the kitchen, and a fairy appeared!

"Don't be afraid, my dear. I am your fairy godmother," she said, "and you shall go to the ball!"

The fairy godmother told Cinderella to find a pumpkin, four white mice, and a black rat. With a wave of her wand, the fairy godmother turned the pumpkin into a golden coach, the four mice into four white horses, and the rat into a coachman.

"How wonderful!" Cinderella cried. "But I can't go to the ball in these rags."

The fairy godmother waved her wand again. Cinderella's rags turned into a beautiful ballgown, and glittering glass slippers appeared on her feet. Cinderella looked lovely!

"Remember—all this will vanish at midnight," said the fairy.

The golden coach whisked Cinderella away to the palace.

Everyone was enchanted by the beautiful stranger, and the prince danced with Cinderella all evening.

Suddenly, the palace clock struck midnight. Cinderella hurried away down the steps, leaving a glass slipper behind

She quickly jumped into the coach, and it drove off.

Soon Cinderella found herself sitting on the road beside a pumpkin, four white mice, and a black rat.

She was dressed in rags and had only one glass slipper left to remember her magical evening.

The prince found the glass slipper on the palace steps. He could not forget the girl he had danced with all night, so he set out to visit every house in the land until he found the girl who fit the shoe.

At last, he came to Cinderella's house. Cinderella scrubbed the floor while she watched her stepsisters try on the glass slipper. But the delicate shoe didn't fit them.

"May I try, please?" asked Cinderella.

"You didn't even go to the ball!" laughed the stepsisters.

"Everyone may try," the prince said.

Cinderella sat down. Her foot slipped easily into the glass slipper.

"It's you!" said the delighted prince. "Will you marry me?"

At that moment, the fairy godmother appeared and turned Cinderella's rags back into a ballgown. Cinderella took the other slipper from her pocket.

"Yes," Cinderella said, "it was me, and yes, I will marry you!"

Cinderella's stepmother and stepsisters were furious.

The couple married the very next day and lived long, happy lives together in the palace.

Meanwhile, Cinderella's mean stepmother and stepsisters had to do their own cleaning, and they never went to another ball at the palace.

Jack and the Beanstalk

Once there was a boy named Jack who lived with his mother. They were very poor and had to sell their cow to get money for food.

On the way to the market, Jack met an old man.

"You won't get much money for such an old cow,"
he told Jack, "but I can give you something better than
money for her—magic beans!"

He held out his hand and showed Jack five speckled
beans.

Magic beans! thought Jack. They sound exciting!

He gave the old man the cow and took the beans,
thanking the man politely. Then he went home.

Jack's mother was extremely cross.

"Silly boy!" she shouted. "Thanks to you, we have no cow and no money!"

She threw the beans out of the window and sent Jack straight to bed.

The next morning, Jack was astonished when he looked out of the window. A giant beanstalk had sprung up while he was sleeping, and it stretched up to the sky.

Jack ran outside and began to climb the beanstalk.

Up and up he went, higher and higher, till he reached the top.

There he found a road, which led to a big castle.

Jack's tummy was rumbling with hunger, so he knocked on the large wooden door.

A giant woman answered. She looked kind, and Jack asked if she would give him some breakfast.

"You will be breakfast if my master finds you!" she told Jack. "He's much bigger than me, and he eats children!"

But Jack begged and pleaded, and at last the giant's cook let him in. She gave him some bread and milk and hid him in a cupboard.

Soon Jack heard loud footsteps and felt the cupboard shake. The giant man was coming! Jack heard him roar,

"Fee-fi-fo-fum, I smell the blood of an Englishman!"

"No, silly," the cook said. "You smell the sausages I've cooked for your breakfast! Now sit down and eat."

After wolfing down three plates of sausages, the giant asked his cook to bring out his gold. She brought two big sacks filled with gold coins, which the giant began to count. But he was sleepy after his big breakfast and soon began to snore.

Jack crept out of the cupboard and grabbed one of the sacks. Then he rushed out of the house, along the road, and down the beanstalk.

Jack's mother was overjoyed to see him, and she was even happier when she saw the gold.

They lived well while the money lasted, but after a year, it had all been spent. Once again, Jack and his mother had nothing to eat.

"Don't worry, Mother," said Jack. "I'll just go back up the beanstalk to the giant's house."

And so he did. Just as before, Jack knocked on the door and begged the giant's cook for something to eat.

"Go away," she told him. "The last time you were here, a sack of gold disappeared. The giant was really cross!"

But once again, Jack begged and pleaded, and at last she let him in. She gave him some bread and milk and hid him in the cupboard.

Soon the giant stomped in, bellowing,

"Fee-fi-fo-fum,
I smell the blood of an Englishman!"

"Nonsense," said the giant's cook. "You smell the soup I've cooked for your lunch."

Peeping through a crack in the cupboard door, Jack saw the giant slurp down a big barrelful of soup and heard him tell the cook,

"Bring me my hen!"

She put a fat red hen
on the table, and the
giant shouted,

"Lay!"

To Jack's amazement, the hen laid a golden egg!

Jack waited until the giant was asleep.

Zzzzzzzz!

Then he jumped out and snatched the hen. Fast as lightning, he dashed out of the house, along the road ...

and

down

the

beanstalk.

43

Jack and his mother lived well on the money they made from the hen's golden eggs. But Jack wanted to climb the beanstalk one last time. He knew the cook would not let him in again, so he sneaked into the house and crawled into the cupboard. Before long, the giant came crashing in.

"Fee-fi-fo-fum, I smell the blood of an Englishman!"

he thundered.

"You smell the steaks I've cooked for your dinner," the cook said. And she put a platter of thick, juicy steaks in front of him.

After gobbling up the steaks, the giant took out a golden harp and said, "Sing!" The harp played a gentle lullaby, and soon the giant was fast asleep.

Jack sprang out, took the harp, and began to run. But the harp cried, "Master! Master!"

... and the giant woke up.
With a roar, he leapt up
and ran after Jack.

Holding the harp tightly, Jack scrambled down the beanstalk. He yelled, "Mother! Bring the ax!"

Jack took the ax and started to chop down the beanstalk.

The giant quickly climbed back up to the top before the beanstalk snapped in two. That was the last time Jack saw him.

With the hen and the harp, Jack and his mother were able to live happily ever after—and they were never hungry again.

Hansel and Gretel

Hansel and Gretel lived at the edge of the forest with their father, a poor woodcutter, and their stepmother.

One night, the family had very little food left to eat.

Hansel and Gretel overheard their father and stepmother talking as they lay in their beds.

"There are too many mouths to feed," said their stepmother. "We must take the children into the forest and leave them there."

"No!" protested the father, for he loved his children.

"We must or we'll all die of hunger!" ordered his wife.

That night, Hansel crept out of the house. He filled his pockets with little white pebbles, then went back to bed.

Early the next morning, the stepmother hurried Hansel and Gretel out of bed.

With a heavy heart, the woodcutter led his children into the forest. As they walked along, Hansel dropped the pebbles from his pockets onto the path.

When they reached the middle of the forest, the woodcutter said, "Wait here. We'll be back soon."

But their father and stepmother didn't return.

Soon it was getting dark. Gretel was frightened.

"We'll find our way home," Hansel told her.

Before long, the moon lit up the white pebbles along the path.

"Don't worry, we'll follow the pebbles home!" said Hansel.

The woodcutter was happy to see his children again, but their stepmother was furious.

After awhile, the woodcutter and his family had very little food again.

"Tomorrow we will take the children deeper into the forest!" the stepmother cried.

This time, Hansel left a trail of breadcrumbs.

When their parents didn't return again, Hansel said, "We'll follow the breadcrumbs I dropped on the path. They will lead us home."

But the birds had eaten all the crumbs.

Tired and hungry, Hansel and Gretel curled up under a tree and went to sleep.

The next morning, they wandered through the forest until they came to a cottage made out of candy and gingerbread. Hansel and Gretel greedily ate the candy.

Suddenly, an old woman opened the door.

"Come in," she said. "I've got more food."

The old woman fed them well and then put them to bed.

Hansel and Gretel didn't know that the old woman was actually a wicked witch who liked to eat children!

51

When Hansel and Gretel woke up, the old woman locked Hansel in a cage. Then the witch set Gretel to work, cooking huge meals to fatten him up.

Every morning, the witch asked Hansel to hold out his finger to feel if he was fat enough to eat.

But clever Hansel held out a chicken bone instead. The witch's eyesight was so bad that she thought it was Hansel's thin finger.

One day, tired of waiting for Hansel to get fatter, the witch decided to cook him anyway.

Grabbing Gretel's arm, she said, "Go and check if the oven is hot enough." And she pushed Gretel toward the open oven door. The wicked witch was planning to eat Gretel, too! But Gretel guessed the witch's trick.

"I'm too big to fit in there," she said.

"Oh, you silly girl," cackled the witch. "Even I can fit in there." And she stuck her head inside. With a great big shove, Gretel pushed the witch into the oven and shut the door.

"The witch is dead!" cried Gretel, and she set Hansel free. As they left, the children discovered the house was full of jewels and gold. So they filled their pockets and set off home.

Their father was overjoyed to see them. He told them that their stepmother had left, and they now had nothing to fear.

Hansel and Gretel showed their father the jewels and gold, and they never went poor or hungry again.

The Princess and the Pea

Once upon a time, there was a lonely prince. He lived in a big castle with beautiful rooms and a pretty garden. But he wasn't happy because he didn't have someone special to share them with.

"If only I could find a lovely princess to marry," sighed the prince.

The king and queen did their best to help. They held balls, so that the prince could meet princesses from all the nearby kingdoms.

The prince danced with tall princesses and small princesses. He talked to loud princesses and proud princesses.

He met all kinds of princesses ... but none of them were quite right.

After awhile, the king and queen ran out of princesses for their son to meet.

"Maybe it's time you went looking for a bride," suggested the queen.

So the prince packed a bag, saddled his horse, and waved goodbye to the king and queen.

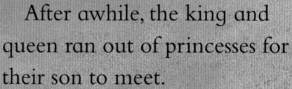

The prince traveled far and wide, and searched high and low for the princess of his dreams. Along the way, he met lots of pretty princesses.

Princess Grace loved to dance, but her twirling made the prince dizzy.

Princess Ginger loved to bake, but her cakes made the prince chubby.

Princess Flora loved to smell as pretty as a flower, but her perfume made the prince sneezy.

ACHOOOO!

Maybe I'm just too fussy, thought the prince. But in his heart, he knew he hadn't met the princess of his dreams. So he headed back to the castle.

When he got home, the king and queen greeted the prince happily.

"I haven't found a princess yet," he sniffed sadly. "I guess I never will."

"Don't be silly," said the queen. "The right girl will come along soon."

That night, there was a terrible storm. Thunder boomed so loudly that it rattled the castle's windows. Lightning shook the table as the prince and his parents sat down to eat their dinner. The prince was just about to help himself to some food when, suddenly, they all heard a loud ...

RAT-A-TAT-TAT!

Someone was knocking on the door!

"Who could be visiting us on a night like this?" asked the queen. The prince opened the door and found a very wet girl stood there. Raindrops ran down her muddy cloak, making a puddle at her feet.

"Hello," the girl said with a smile. "I got lost on my way home and wondered if I could stay here for the night? My name is Princess Polly."

She didn't look much like a princess. But princes must always be polite, so he invited her inside.

Soon the princess was warm and dry.

All night long, rain fell plippety-plop, plippety-plop, on the castle roof. But the prince hardly noticed, because he was too busy talking to Princess Polly.

She was pretty and funny and kind. Princess Polly was everything the prince had hoped to find in a princess.

By the end of the evening, the prince had fallen in love!

But the queen wanted to be sure that the girl really was a princess.

The queen asked the servants to pile a bed high with mattresses. They heaved one on top of another until they had no more mattresses left. Then they placed a pillow and blanket right at the top.

Underneath the mattress at the very bottom, the queen placed a teeny, tiny pea.

Only a real princess would be able to feel something so small through all those mattresses!

When the queen showed Princess Polly to her bedroom, the girl gazed up at the tower of mattresses but didn't say anything. She was just grateful to have a bed for the night.

"Goodnight," said Princess Polly.

"Sleep tight," whispered the queen.

Then Princess Polly changed into her nightgown, climbed to the top of the pile of mattresses, and snuggled under the blanket.

The next morning, Princess Polly came down to breakfast with dark circles under her eyes. She let out a great big yawn.

"How did you sleep, my dear?" asked the queen.

Princess Polly burst into tears.

"I'm afraid I couldn't sleep a wink. There was something lumpy in my bed. It kept me awake all night long!"

To Princess Polly's surprise, the queen clapped her hands with delight.

"She is a real princess!" the queen cried. The prince was overjoyed.

"Will you marry me, Princess Polly?" he asked.

"Yes!" squealed the princess. And they all lived happily ever after!

The Three Billy Goats Gruff

Once upon a time, there were three goats—a little white one, a medium-sized brown one, and a big gray one. They were the Billy Goats Gruff, and they were brothers.

The little Billy Goat Gruff had little horns.

The medium-sized Billy Goat Gruff had medium-sized horns.

And the big Billy Goat Gruff had big, curly horns!

The three brothers lived in a small meadow beside a river.

On the other side of the river, over a bridge, was a huge field with long, juicy grass. But beneath the bridge lived a mean old troll.

He guarded the bridge day and night.

Soon, the grass in the meadow where the three Billy Goats Gruff lived got shorter and drier and browner. The three brothers were getting hungrier and hungrier for fresh, juicy grass.

One day, the little Billy Goat Gruff trotted over the bridge to get to the juicy grass on the other side.

He ran, TRIP-TRAP, TRIP-TRAP, across the bridge.

Suddenly, a croaky voice roared out, "Who's that TRIP-TRAPPING over my bridge? I'll eat you if you pass!"

"Please don't eat me," cried the little goat. He had a plan. "My brother will soon be crossing, and he is much bigger and tastier than me!"

"All right," agreed the greedy troll, and he let the little goat cross.

Later that day, the medium-sized goat saw his little brother munching on the juicy grass on the other side. He wanted to eat it, too.

He turned to the big Billy Goat Gruff. "If he can cross the bridge, then so can I!" he said.

And off he set, TRIP-TRAP, TRIP-TRAP, across the bridge.

Suddenly, the mean troll climbed out from his hiding place.

"Who's that TRIP-TRAPPING over my bridge? I'll eat you if you pass!"

"Please don't eat me," cried the medium-sized goat. "Wait for my brother—he is much bigger and tastier than me."

The troll licked his lips and let the medium-sized goat cross the bridge to join his little brother.

Soon the biggest goat wanted to join his brothers.

So off he set, TRIP-TRAP, TRIP-TRAP, across the bridge.

"Who's that TRIP-TRAPPING over my bridge?" cried the troll. "I'll eat you if you pass!"

The troll's tummy had started rumbling.

"You can't eat me!" shouted the big Billy Goat Gruff, stamping his hooves. "I'm BIG and I have BIG horns!" The big goat put his head down, charged at the troll, and tossed him into the river.

Down, down, down

fell the troll.

With a huge splash, he dropped into the river and floated away.

And that was the end of the mean old troll.

"Well done, big brother!" laughed the little Billy Goat Gruff and the medium-sized Billy Goat Gruff. "Come and eat this juicy grass."

And the troll never bothered the brothers again.

The Elves and the Shoemaker

Once upon a time, a shoemaker lived with his wife above his workshop.

The shoemaker was a good man, and he worked hard, but he was very poor. The day came when he had only enough leather left to make one pair of shoes.

He cut out the leather and then left it on his workbench.

"I will be able to make a better pair of shoes after I've had a good night's sleep," he told his wife as they went upstairs.

The next morning, the shoemaker
went downstairs.

What a surprise he had!

Instead of the leather on his
workbench, there was a brand new
pair of shoes. They were neatly and
perfectly made, with not a stitch out of place.

"These shoes are masterpieces!" the shoemaker exclaimed
to his wife. He put them in the window, hoping someone
would come and buy them.

Soon, a finely dressed young man entered
the workshop to try on the shoes. They fitted
perfectly. The man was so pleased, he happily
paid a high price.

The shoemaker was able
to buy enough leather
to make two new pairs
of shoes. That night, the shoemaker
was tired, so he cut out the leather and left it on his
workbench. Then he went to bed.

The next morning, the shoemaker had
another surprise! There on the workbench
were two new pairs of shoes! They were
even more beautiful than the first pair
and were just as perfectly made.

Before lunchtime, the shoemaker had
sold both pairs for a very good price.

Now he had enough money to buy leather
for four pairs of shoes.

Once again, he cut
out the leather, left it on
his workbench, and went
upstairs to bed.

In the morning, they
found four pairs of shoes,
all perfectly stitched.

The same thing happened every day for weeks. The shoes were appearing as if by magic.

"Let's try and find out who's making them," his wife said.

So that night, the shoemaker left some leather on his workbench, just as before.

Then, instead of going to bed, he and his wife hid behind a curtain at the back of the shop.

There they waited ... and waited ... and waited.

Finally, at the stroke of midnight, in danced two tiny elves through the shop door! They skipped up to the workbench and quickly began sewing the leather into fine new shoes.

As they worked, they sang,

"We will sew and we will stitch, To help the shoemaker grow rich!"

Soon the shoes were finished, and the little elves danced out of the shop.

"We must repay our little helpers for their kindness," the shoemaker told his wife.

"Let's make them some fine clothes," she said.

The next day, the shoemaker's wife knitted two cozy woolen jackets ... two tiny scarves ... and two pairs of warm pants.

The shoemaker used his finest leather to make two little pairs of boots.

That night, instead of leaving leather on his workbench, the shoemaker left the clothes, all wrapped up in shiny paper and ribbons. Then he and his wife hid behind the curtain to wait.

At the stroke of midnight, the shop door opened, and in came the little elves.

They hopped up onto the workbench and saw the presents that had been left for them.

The elves opened the parcels at once, and in the twinkling of an eye, they had dressed in their new clothes.

The presents were the shoemaker's way of saying thank you. The elves did a happy dance, singing,

"Now the shoemaker's grown rich, There's no need to sew and stitch."

Then they hopped off the workbench and scurried out of the door.

The shoemaker and his wife never saw the little elves again. But their troubles were over, and they had a good and happy life together for many long years.

The Big Ship Sails

The big ship sails on the ally-ally-oh,
The ally-ally-oh, the ally-ally-oh.
Oh, the big ship sails on the ally-ally-oh
On the last day of September.

The captain said, "It will never, never do,
Never, never do, never, never do."
The captain said, "It will never, never do."
On the last day of September.

The big ship sank to the bottom of the sea,
The bottom of the sea, the bottom of the sea.
The big ship sank to the bottom of the sea
On the last day of September.

We all dip our heads in the deep blue sea,
The deep blue sea, the deep blue sea.
We all dip our heads in the deep blue sea
On the last day of September.

Five Little Speckled Frogs

Five little speckled frogs,
Sat on a speckled log,
Eating the most delicious bugs,
Yum, yum!
One jumped into the pool,
Where it was nice and cool.
Now there are four green speckled frogs,

Glub, glub!

*(Repeat the rhyme, counting down from five little speckled frogs
to one little speckled frog …)*

One little speckled frog,
Sat on a speckled log,
Eating the most delicious bugs,
Yum, yum!
He jumped into the pool,
Where it was nice and cool.
Now there are no green speckled frogs,

Glub, glub!

Sing a Song of Sixpence

Sing a song of sixpence
A pocket full of rye.
Four and twenty blackbirds
Baked in a pie.
When the pie was opened
The birds began to sing.
Now wasn't that a dainty dish
To set before the king?

The king was in his counting house
Counting out his money.
The queen was in the parlor
Eating bread and honey.
The maid was in the garden
Hanging out the clothes,
When down came a blackbird
And pecked off her nose!

There was a Crooked Man

There was a crooked man
And he walked a crooked mile,
He found a crooked sixpence
Upon a crooked stile.

He bought a crooked cat,
Which caught a crooked mouse,
And they all lived together
In a little crooked house.

Eeny, Meeny

Eeny, meeny, miney, mo,
Catch a tiger by the toe,
If he squeals let him go,
Eeny, meeny, miney, mo.

Old Mother Hubbard

Old Mother Hubbard
Went to the cupboard,
To get her poor doggie a bone.
But when she got there
The cupboard was bare,
So her poor little doggie had none.